D1531511

Where's the Cake?

A HEAD FIRST *Birthday Celebration*

Photographs by
JUDY REINEN
with text by
PATRICK REGAN

Andrews McMeel
Publishing

Kansas City

ISBN: 0-7407-3634-5

05 06 07 08 09 WKT 10 9 8 7 6 5 4 3 2 1

Other  Books

What I Like about You:
A Head First Look at Friendship

ATTENTION: SCHOOLS AND BUSINESSES

Andrews McMeel books are available at quantity discounts with bulk purchase for educational, business, or sales promotional use. For information, please write to: Special Sales Department, Andrews McMeel Publishing, 4520 Main Street, Kansas City, Missouri 64111.

For: Nanay

Happy Birthday!

From: Laura, Liam & Julia

Acknowledgments

I want to thank all our magnificent friends from the animal kingdom who allowed me to look into their eyes and preserve their images for generations to enjoy.

I would also like to thank a number of people and organizations that made the Head First portraits possible by their daily work in the preservation of our animal friends.

Alma Park Zoo, Queensland, Australia
Australian Reptile Park, New South Wales, Australia
Currumbin Wildlife Sanctuary, Queensland, Australia
Denver Zoo, Colorado, United States of America
Mogo Zoo, New South Wales, Australia
Stoney Oaks Wildlife Park, New Zealand
Zion Wildlife Gardens, New Zealand
Brenton Bullen, New South Wales, Australia
Karen Hawkyard, New Zealand

Thank you also to the wonderful owners of all the cats, dogs, and domestic animals I photographed. It's great to work with like-minded people who love animals as much as I do!

Furthermore, I feel extremely honored to have been able to photograph each and every animal in the Head First range. I was blown away by the beauty of these animals while viewing them from an extremely close distance—eight inches to be exact! These animals are so important. It makes you realize the extreme value we must place on ensuring their survival.

God bless,

Judy Reinen, M.Photog NZIPP (2 Gold Bars)

This one's for you, Dad.
Thank you for sharing your love of
photography with me. Wish you
were here to see it.

Why the **LONG** face?

Ahh, yes . . . **ANOTHER BIRTHDAY**
has arrived.

Try to **CONTROL** your excitement.

Another
year
BEHIND
you . . .

and you're not quite sure **WHERE** it's gone.

Well, there are **LOTS** of ways you can approach your birthday.

Some folks try to **IGNORE** it completely.

And some turn up their **NOSES** at the whole idea.

Some make it known that they are not the **LEAST BIT** amused about getting older.

Nope, you can't sneak **PAST** it.

There's nothing to do but grin and **BEAR** it.

After all, you've **EARNED** your stripes.

Look at it **THIS** way:

If **EVERYONE ELSE** is getting older
at exactly the same rate as you are . . .

then—compared to everyone else—you're not **REALLY** getting older, right?

Don't let **THIS** birthday ruffle your feathers.

Focus on the **UPSIDE**.

On your
birthday
you can get
away with
practically
ANYTHING!

You can **SLEEP IN** . . .

eat what you **WANT** . . .

get all **DOLLED** UP . . .

let your hair DOWN . . .

or—if you get a **WILD** hare—

even show a little **SKIN**.

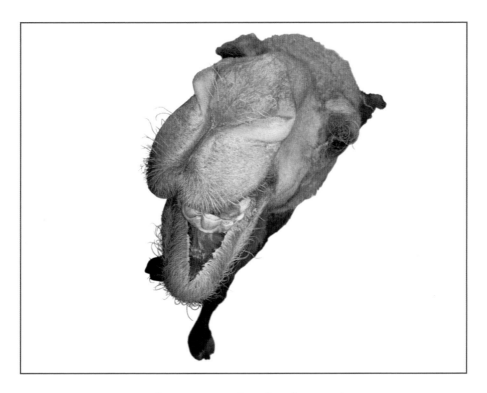

When you think about it,
birthdays offer a **LOT** to smile about. No, really!

After all, you're the same old kid you **ALWAYS** were.

You've just attained a little more life **EXPERIENCE**.

You've learned to **EXPRESS** yourself
clearly and concisely,

and that it's best to tackle problems **HEAD-ON**

You've learned that **SOMETIMES**
a little nap can make all the difference,

that
CHARM
can open
almost any
door,

and that tenacity (and a **LITTLE** attitude) can open the others.

So don't let this birthday **LICK** ya!

And don't let it get your **GOAT**.

REVEL in it!

And accept the adoration of your **FRIENDS** with open arms.

I think I speak for **ALL** of us when I say
that you are a rare breed, indeed.

Getting **OLDER?**

BAH!

You're getting **BETTER** every year!

So Happy Birthday with a big **KISS** from me to you!

Now, **WHERE'S** the cake?